THE LORD'S PRAYER

DOUGLAS CONNELLY

8 STUDIES
FOR INDIVIDUALS
OR GROUPS

ivp

Life
Builder
Study

INTER-VARSITY PRESS
36 Causton Street, London SW1P 4ST, England
Email: ivp@ivpbooks.com
Website: www.ivpbooks.com

*Originally published in the United States of America in the LifeGuide® Bible Studies series
in 2003 by InterVarsity Press, Downers Grove, Illinois*
First published in Great Britain by Scripture Union in 2004
This edition published in Great Britain by Inter-Varsity Press 2018

British Library Cataloguing-in-Publication Data
A catalogue record for this book is available from the British Library.

ISBN: 978–1–78359–803–8

Printed in Great Britain by 4edge Limited

*Inter-Varsity Press publishes Christian books that are true to the Bible and that communicate
the gospel, develop discipleship and strengthen the church for its mission in the world.*

*IVP originated within the Inter-Varsity Fellowship, now the Universities and Colleges Christian
Fellowship, a student movement connecting Christian Unions in universities and colleges
throughout Great Britain, and a member movement of the International Fellowship of
Evangelical Students. Website: www.uccf.org.uk. That historic association is maintained,
and all senior IVP staff and committee members subscribe to the UCCF Basis of Faith.*

Contents

Getting the Most Out of
The Lord's Prayer

No other words of the Bible are spoken more often than the 65 words we call the Lord's Prayer. Countless times every day, in the worship of the church and in the personal devotion of many Christians, these words spring to life—"Our Father, who art in heaven." The prayer is sung, recited in unison, mumbled mindlessly at times and, at other times, choked out through sobs of pain or remorse. For two thousand years Christians on every continent, and in every language, have lifted this prayer to God. When you take these words on your lips, you stand on sacred ground.

But what exactly was Jesus trying to communicate to us when he spoke this prayer? Did he intend that his followers would simply repeat the prayer, or was he giving us a pattern to follow in our own pursuit of prayer—or both? Prayer is one of those aspects of the Christian life that we don't fully understand, and yet Jesus enthusiastically invites us to pray. We can pray about a need for days or years and nothing seems to happen, but Jesus challenges us to keep at it. Prayer takes time and energy and discipline, and yet Jesus, even at his busiest, always put a priority on prayer. Maybe our prayers seem weak and ineffective because we haven't really listened to Jesus or learned from his example.

We call it the Lord's Prayer, but really it is the Disciples' Prayer. Jesus was showing his followers (including us) how to pray. The essential elements are all included. Our prayers simply adapt the requests to fit our own needs and circumstances.

This study guide is designed to help us look carefully at the Lord's Prayer. In the first session we will read through the whole prayer but then focus on what it means to pray to the Father. In the subsequent sessions we will continue through the prayer line by line, drawing in a secondary passage to go deeper into the themes for prayer that Jesus outlined. The goal, however, is not just to know more *about* the prayer; the goal is to begin to pray as Jesus instructed us to pray. Studying the prayer is an important step, but what we want to cultivate is a passion to pray.

Suggestions for Individual Study

1. As you begin each study, pray that God will speak to you through his Word.

2. Read the introduction to the study and respond to the personal reflection question or exercise. This is designed to help you focus on God and on the theme of the study.

3. Each study deals with a particular passage—so that you can delve into the author's meaning in that context. Read and reread the passage to be studied. The questions are written using the language of the New International Version, so you may wish to use that version of the Bible. The New Revised Standard Version is also recommended.

4. This is an inductive Bible study, designed to help you discover for yourself what Scripture is saying. The study includes three types of questions. *Observation* questions ask about the basic facts: who, what, when, where and how. *Interpretation* questions delve into the meaning of the passage. *Application* questions help you discover the implications of the text for growing in Christ. These three keys unlock the treasures of Scripture.

Write your answers to the questions in the spaces provided

or in a personal journal. Writing can bring clarity and deeper understanding of yourself and of God's Word.

5. It might be good to have a Bible dictionary handy. Use it to look up any unfamiliar words, names or places.

6. Use the prayer suggestion to guide you in thanking God for what you have learned and to pray about the applications that have come to mind.

7. You may want to go on to the suggestion under "Now or Later," or you may want to use that idea for your next study.

Suggestions for Members of a Group Study

1. Come to the study prepared. Follow the suggestions for individual study mentioned above. You will find that careful preparation will greatly enrich your time spent in group discussion.

2. Be willing to participate in the discussion. The leader of your group will not be lecturing. Instead, he or she will be encouraging the members of the group to discuss what they have learned. The leader will be asking the questions that are found in this guide.

3. Stick to the topic being discussed. Your answers should be based on the verses which are the focus of the discussion and not on outside authorities such as commentaries or speakers. These studies focus on a particular passage of Scripture. Only rarely should you refer to other portions of the Bible. This allows for everyone to participate in in-depth study on equal ground.

4. Be sensitive to the other members of the group. Listen attentively when they describe what they have learned. You may be surprised by their insights! Each question assumes a variety of answers. Many questions do not have "right" answers, particularly questions that aim at meaning or application. Instead the questions push us to explore the passage more thoroughly.

When possible, link what you say to the comments of others. Also, be affirming whenever you can. This will encourage some of the more hesitant members of the group to participate.

5. Be careful not to dominate the discussion. We are sometimes so eager to express our thoughts that we leave too little opportunity for others to respond. By all means participate! But allow others to also.

6. Expect God to teach you through the passage being discussed and through the other members of the group. Pray that you will have an enjoyable and profitable time together, but also that as a result of the study you will find ways that you can take action individually and/or as a group.

7. Remember that anything said in the group is considered confidential and should not be discussed outside the group unless specific permission is given to do so.

8. If you are the group leader, you will find additional suggestions at the back of the guide.

1

Talking to the Father

Matthew 6:5-15

When I was about fifteen years old, our family visited some caverns in Pennsylvania. At every stop on the tour the guide droned on and on about stalagmites and rock formations while I just wanted to see what was next. At one point I left the lecture and moved ahead on the trail. What I didn't know was that the guide was about to turn off all the lights in the cave so we could experience absolute darkness. When the lights went off, I was so frightened I opened my mouth to let out a scream. At that moment a hand touched my shoulder and a familiar voice said, "Doug, I'm right here." My dad had seen me walk away and had followed. It was still dark, but I felt safe in my father's care.

GROUP DISCUSSION. Talk about one positive quality that you saw in your father or that you imagine in an ideal father.

PERSONAL REFLECTION. If you could fashion a father, what one character trait would be most important?

What we have come to call the Lord's Prayer was spoken in the middle of Jesus' Sermon on the Mount—a long talk Jesus gave about how to live distinctively as a Christian in an evil world. Jesus gave the prayer to his followers in the context of some very practical words on when and where and how to pray. We will read the whole prayer but focus on verses 5-9 in this session. *Read Matthew 6:5-15.*

1. What kinds of dysfunctional prayer does Jesus warn about in verses 5-8?

2. Jesus commands us to pray in secret. Does that rule out public prayer? Explain your answer.

3. When you pray out loud in front of other people, what can you do to focus on God rather than on how your prayer sounds to others?

4. Since we are not to pray repetitive ("babbling") prayers (v. 7), how can you make repeating the Lord's Prayer spiritually enriching?

5. If God knows our needs before we pray (v. 8), why pray at all?

---

6. As you think about the context in which the Lord's Prayer was first spoken (skim chapters 5 and 6), do you think Jesus wanted us to pray these exact words, or is he giving us a general pattern for prayer? Why?

What misuses of the prayer could spring from either position?

---

7. The word Jesus uses to call on the Father is the common word that children in Jesus' day used to address their father— the word *Abba*, meaning "Dearest Father." What emotions do you feel as you call God "Dearest Father"?

---

8. Why does Jesus instruct us to address God as *our* Father rather than *my* Father (v. 9)?

9. If the word *Father* suggests the nearness of God, "Our Father *in heaven*" points to God's majesty and power. How does the fact that God rules in heaven over all things make you feel about coming to him with your needs and requests?

10. Do most of your prayers emphasize God's gentle presence with us or God's awesome majesty?

What can you do to bring more balance in your approach to God in prayer?

Before you pray, reflect quietly for a few minutes on the person you are going to speak to. Think about his greatness, his wisdom and his love. Focus on God and then express your love for him.

Now or Later

The New Testament encourages Christians to address God as *Abba.* Think about your own view of God the Father as you read these verses.

Because you are sons, God sent the Spirit of his Son into our hearts, the Spirit who calls out, "*Abba*, Father." (Galatians 4:6)

For you did not receive a spirit that makes you a slave again to fear, but you received the Spirit of sonship. And by him we cry, "*Abba*, Father." The Spirit himself testifies with our spirit that we are God's children. (Romans 8:15-16)

For the next week address your prayers to *Abba*. It may seem strange at first, but you are taking on your lips the same word Jesus used as he addressed his own dear Father.

2

Showing Some Respect

Isaiah 6:1-8

His mother straightened his tie and brushed imaginary dust off the shoulders of his jacket. Dad stood behind him and smiled. The young man was about to receive several honors as part of his graduating class. "Remember you are our son," his mom said. "Do us proud tonight." Their son's achievement brought honor to the whole family.

GROUP DISCUSSION. Climb back through the branches of your family tree. Were there some relatives who brought honor to your family name? What about one or two who brought dishonor? Tell one of your family stories.

PERSONAL REFLECTION. Proverbs 22:1 says: "A good name is more desirable than great riches." What do you do consistently that enhances the reputation of your name?

The second line of the Lord's Prayer is "Hallowed be your name" (Matthew 6:9). God's *name* in the Bible is the summation of God's character, the fullness of who God is. The word *hallow* means to set apart as sacred and pure, to honor. So the person who prays, "Hallowed be your name," is asking that God's awesome and holy character would be on display to the world.

---

1. Donald Williams writes this: "In general, the glory of God is to be the first thing on our minds when we pray."* What is the first thing we usually focus on in prayer?

---

2. If you pray "Hallowed be your name," you are also offering yourself as a channel through which God can show his holy nature to a drifting and at times rebellious culture. What are some ways that we as Christians can honor God's name in our daily lives?

The Old Testament prophet Isaiah caught a glimpse of God's holy character one day. The king of Judah had died, and the young prophet found himself feeling insecure and fearful. Then he saw the Lord, holy and exalted, and it changed his life. *Read Isaiah 6:1-8.*

---

3. If you were given this vision, how would each of your senses—sight, sound, smell, taste, touch—be affected?

4. What aspects of God's character are emphasized in this vision?

5. Why does Isaiah respond by saying, "I am a man of unclean lips, and I live among a people of unclean lips" (v. 5)?

6. God responds to Isaiah's confession with an act of cleansing. How do you think Isaiah feels after the burning coal experience?

7. If you have had an experience in which you had an overwhelming sense of God's glory and your own weakness and failure, explain what changes that crisis made in your life. (If you have not had such an experience, how will reading about Isaiah's vision change you?)

8. God's cleansing also produces a heart of obedience in Isaiah (v. 8). What is God asking you to do?

9. What will it cost to say, "Here I am. Send me"?

10. What (if anything) will be different in your life tomorrow because you begin to pray: "May my whole life be an honor to your name, Father—hallowed be your name"?

Pray rejoicing that God our Father is the Holy One, the one exalted above everyone and everything else.

Now or Later

The seraphs in Isaiah's vision are angels—powerful spirit beings who are positioned above God's throne to exalt and honor God alone. Use the seraph's words in prayer as an expression of your own praise and adoration to him. Several hymns and praise songs have been written based on the seraph's words. Learn one, and sing it to God as you visualize his awesome majesty.

*Donald Williams, *The Disciples' Prayer* (Camp Hill, Penn.: Christian Publications, 1999), p. 35.

3

Who's Really in Charge?

Matthew 25:31-46

We sometimes think that New Testament Christians were super-saints who never wavered in their faith—until we read the New Testament. As Acts 12 opens, for example, the apostle Peter is in prison and scheduled to be executed the next day. The other Christians are together in a home, praying for Peter's release. When an angel sets Peter free, he immediately goes to the house where the Christians are praying to tell them the good news. He is greeted at the locked door by a servant girl who, in her excitement, runs to tell everyone that the prayer meeting is over. Peter is free! But the Christians say, "Don't interrupt our prayer meeting. It can't be Peter." She persists, however, and Peter keeps knocking until they open the door— and they are astonished. Sounds like our prayers, doesn't it? We pray, but our expectation that God will answer isn't there.

GROUP DISCUSSION. Do our prayers (both in public and in private) usually reflect our will or God's will? How can you tell the difference?

PERSONAL REFLECTION. Think about some of the things you have asked from God lately. Have you ever thanked him for the times he has said "no" to the things you thought were best at the time?

We think of earthly kingdoms in terms of territory—an empire. In the New Testament the kingdom of God is not territory. The term is used to describe the reign of God. God's kingdom today extends over the hearts of all who will acknowledge him as king and who will submit to his rule. They are the same people who desire God's will in every area of life. To pray "your kingdom come" is to ask God the Father to expand his rule over the territory of our hearts and lives; to pray "Your will be done" (Matthew 6:10) is to express our willingness to submit to his rule whatever the cost.

1. What aspects of our personal kingdoms are difficult to submit to God's rule and authority?

2. What do you expect to happen when you pray, "Your will be done on earth as it is in heaven" (Matthew 6:10)?

3. Is this a prayer for God's will to be done in our society as a whole or for God's will to be done in our individual lives—or both? Explain why you came to your conclusion.

The kingdom of God has both a present phase—Christ reigning in our hearts—and a future phase—Christ reigning over the earth at his return. Jesus talked about those who will enter his future kingdom and those who won't. *Read Matthew 25:31-46.*

---

4. What six actions will Jesus use as the basis for his judgment?

---

5. What thoughts and feelings surface as you read about the sheep and the goats (vv. 32-33)?

---

6. Do you think Jesus is teaching that we gain entrance into his kingdom by good works rather than by faith? Explain your answer.

---

7. Which of the actions in verses 34-36 do you find easiest or most natural to do?

Which are most difficult for you?

8. Who is Jesus referring to when he says, "the least of these brothers of mine" (v. 40)?

---

9. If these actions are the marks of kingdom-seekers, what will change in your life as you pray, "Your kingdom come"?

---

10. In heaven God's name is honored, God's reign is supreme, and God's will is carried out fervently and willingly. Our prayer is that the same would be true on earth. What resources do you have available that you can use to do God's will toward someone in need this week?

Pray David's prayer in Psalm 40:8—"I desire to do your will, O my God."

Now or Later

Involve your family or small group in an act of kindness and sacrifice. Volunteer at a rescue mission or food bank. Take a meal to someone who is sick or lonely. Pool your money and buy some clothes for a young person or child who needs them. Remind each other that you are doing these things to extend the reign of God in your hearts and in your community.

4

Why Pray
When You Can Worry?

Luke 12:22-34

When my dad was in college, he heard lots of other students get up in chapel and talk about their "mailbox miracles." They needed money for tuition or rent or even their next meal, and that day a check arrived in the mail from some distant relative. My dad never had that experience. As he tells it, whenever he needed money, God sent him a job! But, whether through mailbox miracles or regular work, God provides.

GROUP DISCUSSION. Relate a story of God's provision in your life or in a friend's life.

PERSONAL REFLECTION. What kinds of issues prompt you to worry most?

The first three requests in the Lord's Prayer focus on the Father—his name, his reign, his will. Most of our prayers start in the middle of this prayer—with our own needs. Jesus doesn't ignore our needs. He just puts them in the right priority. So we turn to the request, "Give us today our daily bread" (Matthew 6:11).

---

1. Jesus instructs us to ask the Father for each day's provision. Why such an emphasis on the immediate—why not ask for a month of groceries?

---

2. Do you think food is the only provision covered in this request? What other necessities might we ask the Father to give us on a daily basis?

Most of the time we don't think much about daily bread. In fact, we're trying to eat less, not more. But when our jobs are cut in a corporate downscale, or when a dip in the stock market threatens our retirement savings or when unexpected demands stretch our financial resources, it's easy to worry. We know God provides; we're just afraid that he won't be there for the crisis we are facing right now. *Read Luke 12:22-34.*

---

3. On a scale of one (representing "no problems") to ten (representing "panic"), what would you register on the worry chart today? Explain why you gave yourself that rating.

4. Does Jesus mean, in verse 22, that we shouldn't plan what to feed our family tomorrow or pick out clothes for work the night before? What *does* he mean?

5. How does worry affect your sense of worth before God (v. 22)?

6. What practical truths can you learn from the ravens (v. 24) and the lilies (vv. 27-28)?

7. How would you use these verses to encourage someone who has just lost a job?

8. How do people who live without faith in God ("the pagan world," v. 30) deal with their daily needs?

Why can Christians respond differently?

9. Verse 31 instructs us to "seek his kingdom." What are some practical ways that you can invest in God's kingdom?

10. If you genuinely adopt the attitude reflected in verses 32-34, how will it change your view of life and your material needs?

Express your dependence on God for all the necessities of life.

Now or Later

Some interpreters of the Lord's Prayer see the phrase "Give us today our daily bread" as a request for spiritual food rather than physical food. Augustine, a church leader in the fifth century, wrote: "It is a prayer for spiritual food, namely, the divine precepts which we are to think over and put into practice each day." E. V. Rieu translates the phrase: "Give us the bread of life today." Jesus said, "I am the bread of life. He who comes to me will never go hungry" (John 6:35). How do you pray for spiritual nourishment?

Where do you go to find that kind of "bread"?

5

Costly Forgiveness

Dawn Smith Jordan learned about forgiveness the hard way. In 1985 her seventeen-year-old sister, Sherrie, was abducted and murdered. After her body was found, the killer phoned the family several times and described in detail how he had killed Sherrie. In time, the murderer was caught and sentenced to death. Dawn and her family thought the story was finally over.

The story wasn't over, however. A few years later the convicted murderer wrote Dawn's family a letter and told them he had become a Christian. His next question was the hard one: "Will you ever forgive me for what I've done?"

GROUP DISCUSSION. Put yourself in that family's place. How would you respond to the killer's letter?

PERSONAL REFLECTION. In what situations do you find it most difficult to forgive?

The fifth request in the Lord's Prayer is for forgiveness. Jesus knew that we would stand in need of forgiveness every day. And so we pray, "Forgive us our debts, as we also have forgiven our debtors" (Matthew 6:12).

---

1. When you ask God to forgive you for a sin or failure in your life, are you confident of his cleansing or do you have doubts? Explain why you feel secure or insecure.

---

2. Christians believe that we receive forgiveness from God by grace alone. Why, in this request, does Jesus make it sound like our forgiveness of others is a condition for our forgiveness from God? (Read Matthew 6:14-15 for further clarification on Jesus' position.)

---

3. What price did God pay to forgive us?

What price do we pay when we forgive others?

Peter tried to impress Jesus one day with his willingness to forgive other people up to seven times. Jesus wasn't impressed. Genuine forgiveness doesn't keep a record, and genuine forgivers don't keep count. *Read Matthew 18:21-35.*

---

4. Who is the easiest person for you to forgive? Why?

Who is the hardest person for you to forgive and why?

---

5. The servant in Jesus' parable owed his king two billion dollars, and the master forgave his debt. The servant's coworker owed him twenty dollars, and he demanded repayment. What do the sizes of the two debts show you about the comparison of our debt of sin to God and the debt of hurt we are owed from others?

---

6. What does the servant's attitude toward the man who owed him money tell you about his response to the king's gracious forgiveness of him?

7. Do you think you would have responded to the fellow servant in the same way? Rewrite the dialogue in verses 28-30 to reflect what you would say.

8. How does Jesus apply the parable to us (v. 35)?

Does this mean that God will take away our forgiveness if we refuse to forgive others? Explain your answer.

9. Some people find it is better to address strained relationships after they have had some time to calm down and reflect. Other people like to deal with the problem right away. What methods have you found helpful in dealing with problems in your relationships?

10. What are some specific ways that you can demonstrate that you are a forgiven person?

11. How will this parable change the way you relate to the person you find hardest to forgive?

Confess any area of sin or disobedience to God, and receive his forgiveness. Ask God to help you remember this week how much he has forgiven you.

Now or Later

Dawn's family eventually did come to the place of forgiveness. She gave this testimony: "It wasn't easy. It wasn't overnight. But God gave the answer that I needed. We are to forgive just as Jesus forgave us. I was finally able to sit down and write the man who murdered my sister a letter telling him that only because of the grace I have received in my life could I let him know that he was forgiven."*

Think of a person in your family or church fellowship who models a forgiving spirit. Take that person to lunch or out for coffee and ask them how they have cultivated that spirit. If the person is reluctant to talk about it, share some of your own struggles with forgiveness and then ask them for insight and direction.

---

*This account comes from Dawn Smith Jordan's personal story quoted in Robert Jeffress, *When Forgiveness Doesn't Make Sense* (Colorado Springs, Colo.: Waterbrook, 2000), pp. 19-20.

6

Tackling Temptation

She didn't even look when she pulled her car out in front of us. She had stopped at the red light but didn't seem too concerned about the traffic headed toward her. She calmly cut across three lanes of panicked drivers and squealing tires.

That incident on the road presented me with several options. I could indulge in an expression of anger and even shout at the driver through closed windows. Or I could refuse the temptation to say the first thing that came to mind. I could even thank God that no one was hurt.

But before I gave it much thought, I had uttered some choice words for that driver—words I would have to apologize to my son for saying and words I would have to confess later to God.

When I told a friend later about my outburst, he said, "That's what anyone would have done in the same situation. Don't be so hard on yourself." But I wonder if that's not just an excuse. I wonder if Jesus would have reacted that way.

GROUP DISCUSSION. What is the "pet peeve" that gets you upset most quickly?

PERSONAL REFLECTION. In what circumstances do you find it

easiest to let your "before Jesus" nature take control? What excuses do you make for your behavior?

The next two phrases in the Lord's Prayer fit together: "Lead us not into temptation, but deliver us from the evil one" (Matthew 6:13). The word *temptation* can mean to entice to do wrong, but it can also mean to put to the test. The same experience can be both a temptation to do wrong and a test of our commitment to do right. Satan, the evil one, wants us to fail the test and sin; God gives us everything we need to pass the test and, as a result, strengthen our walk of obedience.

1. Are there people in your life who you think are above or immune from the enticement to do wrong? How do you feel when you're around them?

2. The New Testament letter of James says: "When tempted, no one should say, 'God is tempting me.' For God cannot be tempted by evil, nor does he tempt anyone" (James 1:13). Why pray that God would not lead us into temptation when he doesn't tempt us to sin anyway?

3. Jesus makes it clear that we need God's power to face temptation and to stand against Satan's attacks. What are some practical ways God might answer these requests in your life?

On the night of his betrayal and arrest, Jesus asked the Father to protect his followers from spiritual attack. *Read John 17:6-19.*

4. What did Jesus' followers know for certain about Jesus and about their own relationship with God (vv. 6-10)?

5. What was Jesus' role in the spiritual protection of his followers during his time on earth (vv. 11-12)?

How would that role change?

6. What resources for spiritual defense are provided for Jesus' disciples to draw on (vv. 14-17)?

7. What suggestions can you draw from verses 14-17 that will help a friend struggling with some temptation in his or her life?

8. It seems that life would be a lot easier if Jesus would just take us out of the world or keep us totally protected from testing or temptation. What would be the results of those options?

9. The word *sanctify* (vv. 17-19) means to be reserved for God—to be separated from sin and evil and to be set apart completely for God. What would mark a Christian as being sanctified?

_____

10. Jesus has sent you out into the world (vv. 18-19). What confidence does this prayer give you as you face your world?

_____

11. As you face temptation, how does it make you feel to know that Jesus is praying for your success to resist its power?

Thank Jesus for praying for you and for the power he provides to live a life of success over temptation.

Now or Later
Since Jesus is praying this prayer for all those who believe in him (v. 20), read John 17:6-19 again but substitute your name for the words *they, them* and *their.* Read each phrase out loud if possible. Think about each statement. Let Jesus' declarations motivate you to a walk of deeper commitment to him.

7

The Power and Glory

Revelation 4

At Princess Diana's funeral in 1997, the worship leader invited the congregation in the cathedral and those millions watching by television to pray the Lord's Prayer in their own language. Someone observed later that more people were praying the Lord's Prayer in more languages at the same time than ever before in history.

A few weeks ago I bent over the bed of a hospice patient who was near death. "Is there anything I can do for you?" I asked. "Pray the Lord's Prayer with me" came the whispered reply. So two people prayed the Lord's Prayer together at the same time—and God was as present as if hundreds had been gathered in that room.

GROUP DISCUSSION. When and where was your most meaningful worship experience? Try to put into words what you heard and felt and saw.

PERSONAL REFLECTION. Think about your last worship experience in church or with other Christians. Who were you focused on most during worship: the people around you? the people up front? yourself? God?

The final sentence of the Lord's Prayer—"For thine is the kingdom, and the power, and the glory, for ever. Amen" (Matthew 6:13 KJV)—is not in the earliest copies of the Gospel of Matthew. In most modern translations of the Bible (like the New International Version) the verse is not included in the main text but appears in a footnote. Most Bible scholars believe that these words were not part of the original prayer Jesus gave his disciples. The phrase was likely added by early Christians as the prayer began to be used in public worship.

So should we include this last sentence as part of the Lord's Prayer or not? My suggestion is that we accept these final words for what they are—not the words of Jesus to us but the words of Jesus' early followers in response to the prayer. The prayer as it stands never really concludes; it just stops. It is almost as if Jesus deliberately left it open-ended—as if he wanted to give us the opportunity to respond spontaneously to the prayer. The response of the early Christians was worship and adoration.

---

1. What does it mean to you personally when you say to God: yours is the kingdom (the right to rule)?

yours is the power (the ability to protect, the strength to do whatever you desire)?

yours is the glory (majesty, infinite worth)?

God's character will never change. He will be the great and good God that he is forever—and all eternity will be centered on the worship of God. In Revelation 4, the apostle John is transported to heaven in a vision, and he sees a magnificent scene. *Read Revelation 4.*

2. If you could take just one snapshot of this unfolding scene, what scene would you capture and why?

3. John sees a figure seated on the throne—a figure representing God the Father. Drawing on this passage, how would you describe God to a friend?

4. The twenty-four elders in the vision (v. 4) represent the people of God, those who have linked themselves to God through faith in Jesus. What is their role in this scene?

5. As you envision a world where God's glory and God's honor cover everything, what in our present experience would be missing from such a world?

6. In your mind, project this scene from Revelation 4 above your personal worship or above your worship in a church service. How will it change your attitude and approach to worship?

_____

7. What would this scene mean to the persecuted Christians who were the first readers of the book—or to persecuted Christians in our world today?

_____

8. What does this vision say to us as we view our threatening and seemingly out-of-control world?

_____

9. The focus of heavenly worship is our awesome God. What can you do to make him more the focus of your personal worship?

What can you do to focus more fully on God when you join in worship with other Christians?

Pray Revelation 4:11 as the expression of your own exaltation of God.

Now or Later

Use your gifts and imagination to give expression to Revelation 4—write a song, paint or draw one of the scenes, compose a drama or a choral reading. Use the artistic or imaginative abilities that God has given you to express your praise to God. Do you think God is pleased with creative expressions of worship? What is he examining as you paint or sing or dance before him?

8

A Passion for Prayer

Luke 11:1-13

Every wedding I've ever been to has included an interesting question: "Do you take this person to have and to hold from this day forward?" The answer always comes back the same: "I do."

Jesus' prayer ends with the little word *Amen*. It's not just the signal that prayer is over. It means, "So be it," and it's a lot like saying "I do" at a wedding. Agreeing to the marriage vows is not the end of our commitment but the beginning. Saying *Amen* at the end of prayer is a commitment to do what we've prayed. We aren't just putting a period at the end of a list of requests; we are making a promise to live out what we've said to God. Be careful with that little word! When you say it, you've just said "I do" to God.

GROUP DISCUSSION. Are you a "plan-and-prepare" person or do you like to be more spontaneous? Give an example of your personal style.

When it comes to prayer, do you usually pray at a set time each day or is your prayer life more of a spontaneous conversation with God?

PERSONAL REFLECTION. What activity most often leads you into genuine prayer—reading the Bible? following a devotional book? listening to or singing music? hearing about someone in need?

The Sermon on the Mount wasn't the only time Jesus gave the Lord's Prayer as instruction to his followers. Luke records an occasion when Jesus' disciples came upon Jesus in prayer, and they asked him to teach them to pray. *Read Luke 11:1-13.*

1. As you read through this version of the Lord's Prayer, what differences do you see from the version we have been studying in Matthew 6:9-13?

2. On a human level, what is the point of the parable in verses 5-8?

3. How do you react to someone's relentless requests for something?

4. Jesus wants to emphasize that God is *not* like the grumpy neighbor who has to be harassed into helping us. How would you characterize God's responsiveness to us based on verses 9-10?

5. How is it possible to misuse or abuse the promises in verses 9-10?

6. What is Jesus' point in the story about fathers and children (vv. 11-13)?

7. Jesus wants us to realize that God is *not* a gruesome father. And yet we may have felt he is at times. Have you ever felt that when you asked God for a fish (something you thought was good and right), he instead gave you a snake (something that ended up being bad and hurtful)? Explain your answer.

What part of Jesus' teaching in these verses will help us to view those situations through God's eyes?

8. Based on this passage in Luke, what would you say to a friend who has prayed about a specific issue for a long time but has not yet seen God respond?

9. As Jesus has "taught you to pray" over the course of this study, what has changed in your approach and attitude toward prayer?

How has your view of God changed or been made clearer?

Pray Luke's version of the Lord's Prayer out loud—individually or as a group.

Now or Later

Use Luke's version of the Lord's Prayer to evaluate how your prayer life has changed during this study. Consider what you are learning in each area. You may want to add items under each heading.

"Father, hallowed be your name"
I spend time exalting and honoring God as my gracious Father and majestic Lord.

"Your kingdom come"
I spend time welcoming God's rule to be extended in my life and in my world.

"Give us each day our daily bread"
I am expressing my trust for God's provision in my life.

"Forgive us our sins"
I consistently ask for and receive God's forgiveness. I am quick to forgive those who have hurt me.

"Lead us not into temptation"
I listen to God's warnings about areas of vulnerability in my life and seek his protection.

Ask God to continue to teach you how to pray.

Leader's Notes

Leading a Bible discussion can be an enjoyable and rewarding experience. But it can also be *scary*—especially if you've never done it before. If this is your feeling, you're in good company. When God asked Moses to lead the Israelites out of Egypt, he replied, "O Lord, please send someone else to do it"! (Ex 4:13). It was the same with Solomon, Jeremiah and Timothy, but God helped these people in spite of their weaknesses, and he will help you as well.

You don't need to be an expert on the Bible or a trained teacher to lead a Bible discussion. The idea behind these inductive studies is that the leader guides group members to discover for themselves what the Bible has to say. This method of learning will allow group members to remember much more of what is said than a lecture would.

These studies are designed to be led easily. As a matter of fact, the flow of questions through the passage from observation to interpretation to application is so natural that you may feel that the studies lead themselves. This study guide is also flexible. You can use it with a variety of groups—student, professional, neighborhood or church groups. Each study takes forty-five to sixty minutes in a group setting.

There are some important facts to know about group dynamics and encouraging discussion. The suggestions listed below should enable you to effectively and enjoyably fulfill your role as leader.

Preparing for the Study

1. Ask God to help you understand and apply the passage in your

46 —————————————————————————————————*The Lord's Prayer*

own life. Unless this happens, you will not be prepared to lead others. Pray too for the various members of the group. Ask God to open your hearts to the message of his Word and motivate you to action.

2. Read the introduction to the entire guide to get an overview of the entire book and the issues which will be explored.

3. As you begin each study, read and reread the assigned Bible passage to familiarize yourself with it.

4. This study guide is based on the New International Version of the Bible. It will help you and the group if you use this translation as the basis for your study and discussion.

5. Carefully work through each question in the study. Spend time in meditation and reflection as you consider how to respond.

6. Write your thoughts and responses in the space provided in the study guide. This will help you to express your understanding of the passage clearly.

7. It might help to have a Bible dictionary handy. Use it to look up any unfamiliar words, names or places. (For additional help on how to study a passage, see chapter five of *How to Lead a LifeBuilder Study,* IVP, 2018.)

8. Consider how you can apply the Scripture to your life. Remember that the group will follow your lead in responding to the studies. They will not go any deeper than you do.

9. Once you have finished your own study of the passage, familiarize yourself with the leader's notes for the study you are leading. These are designed to help you in several ways. First, they tell you the purpose the study guide author had in mind when writing the study. Take time to think through how the study questions work together to accomplish that purpose. Second, the notes provide you with additional background information or suggestions on group dynamics for various questions. This information can be useful when people have difficulty understanding or answering a question. Third, the leader's notes can alert you to potential problems you may encounter during the study.

10. If you wish to remind yourself of anything mentioned in the leader's notes, make a note to yourself below that question in the study.

Leading the Study

1. Begin the study on time. Open with prayer, asking God to help the group to understand and apply the passage.

2. Be sure that everyone in your group has a study guide. Encourage the group to prepare beforehand for each discussion by reading the introduction to the guide and by working through the questions in the study.

3. At the beginning of your first time together, explain that these studies are meant to be discussions, not lectures. Encourage the members of the group to participate. However, do not put pressure on those who may be hesitant to speak during the first few sessions. You may want to suggest the following guidelines to your group.

☐ Stick to the topic being discussed.

☐ Your responses should be based on the verses which are the focus of the discussion and not on outside authorities such as commentaries or speakers.

☐ These studies focus on a particular passage of Scripture. Only rarely should you refer to other portions of the Bible. This allows for everyone to participate in in-depth study on equal ground.

☐ Anything said in the group is considered confidential and will not be discussed outside the group unless specific permission is given to do so.

☐ We will listen attentively to each other and provide time for each person present to talk.

☐ We will pray for each other.

4. Have a group member read the introduction at the beginning of the discussion.

5. Every session begins with a group discussion question. The question or activity is meant to be used before the passage is read. The question introduces the theme of the study and encourages group members to begin to open up. Encourage as many members as possible to participate, and be ready to get the discussion going with your own response.

This section is designed to reveal where our thoughts or feelings need to be transformed by Scripture. That is why it is especially important not to read the passage before the discussion question is asked. The passage will tend to color the honest reactions people would otherwise give because they are, of course, supposed to think the way the Bible does.

You may want to supplement the group discussion question with an icebreaker to help people to get comfortable. See the community section of the *Small Group Starter Kit* (IVP, 1995) for more ideas.

You also might want to use the personal reflection question with your group. Either allow a time of silence for people to respond individually or discuss it together.

6. Have a group member (or members if the passage is long) read aloud the passage to be studied. Then give people several minutes to read the passage again silently so that they can take it all in.

7. Question 1 will generally be an overview question designed to briefly survey the passage. Encourage the group to look at the whole passage, but try to avoid getting sidetracked by questions or issues that will be addressed later in the study.

8. As you ask the questions, keep in mind that they are designed to be used just as they are written. You may simply read them aloud. Or you may prefer to express them in your own words.

There may be times when it is appropriate to deviate from the study guide. For example, a question may have already been answered. If so, move on to the next question. Or someone may raise an important question not covered in the guide. Take time to discuss it, but try to keep the group from going off on tangents.

9. Avoid answering your own questions. If necessary, repeat or rephrase them until they are clearly understood. Or point out something you read in the leader's notes to clarify the context or meaning. An eager group quickly becomes passive and silent if they think the leader will do most of the talking.

10. Don't be afraid of silence. People may need time to think about the question before formulating their answers.

11. Don't be content with just one answer. Ask, "What do the rest of you think?" or "Anything else?" until several people have given answers to the question.

12. Acknowledge all contributions. Try to be affirming whenever possible. Never reject an answer. If it is clearly off-base, ask, "Which verse led you to that conclusion?" or again, "What do the rest of you think?"

13. Don't expect every answer to be addressed to you, even though this will probably happen at first. As group members become more at ease, they will begin to truly interact with each other. This is one sign of healthy discussion.

14. Don't be afraid of controversy. It can be very stimulating. If you don't resolve an issue completely, don't be frustrated. Move on and keep it in mind for later. A subsequent study may solve the problem.

15. Periodically summarize what the group has said about the passage. This helps to draw together the various ideas mentioned and gives continuity to the study. But don't preach.

16. At the end of the Bible discussion you may want to allow group members a time of quiet to work on an idea under "Now or Later." Then discuss what you experienced. Or you may want to encourage group members to work on these ideas between meetings. Give an opportunity during the session for people to talk about what they are learning.

17. Conclude your time together with conversational prayer, adapting the prayer suggestion at the end of the study to your group. Ask for God's help in following through on the commitments you've made.

18. End on time.

Many more suggestions and helps are found in *How to Lead a LifeBuilder Study.*

Components of Small Groups

A healthy small group should do more than study the Bible. There are four components to consider as you structure your time together.

Nurture. Small groups help us to grow in our knowledge and love of God. Bible study is the key to making this happen and is the foundation of your small group.

Community. Small groups are a great place to develop deep friendships with other Christians. Allow time for informal interaction before and after each study. Plan activities and games that will help you get to know each other. Spend time having fun together—going on a picnic or cooking dinner together.

Worship and prayer. Your study will be enhanced by spending time praising God together in prayer or song. Pray for each other's needs—and keep track of how God is answering prayer in your group. Ask God to help you to apply what you are learning in your study.

Outreach. Reaching out to others can be a practical way of applying what you are learning, and it will keep your group from becoming self-focused. Host a series of evangelistic discussions for your friends or neighbors. Clean up the yard of an elderly friend. Serve at a soup kitchen together, or spend a day working in the community.

Many more suggestions and helps in each of these areas are found in the *Small Group Starter Kit*. You will also find information on building a small group. Reading through the starter kit will be worth your time.

General Introduction. The challenge of a study on the Lord's Prayer is to translate the teaching of the passage into our actual practice of prayer. You as a leader can ask one question at some point in every study: How will what Jesus said change the way we pray?

Several excellent books have been written on the Lord's Prayer. Most commentaries on the Gospel of Matthew cover it too. You might want to read through one of these suggested resources before the study begins to give yourself a foundation from which to lead the group.

John MacArthur Jr., *Jesus' Pattern of Prayer* (Moody Press, 1981).

William Barclay, *The Lord's Prayer* (Westminster John Knox, reprint 1998).

Brian J. Dodd, *Praying Jesus' Way* (InterVarsity Press, 1997).

James Mulholland, *Praying Like Jesus* (HarperSanFrancisco, 2001).

I have referred to this prayer by its traditional title—the Lord's Prayer. Many interpreters have pointed out that Jesus himself would never have prayed the full prayer. Since Jesus lived perfectly before the Father, he never had to ask for forgiveness for sin or moral error. The prayer is more accurately called the Disciples' Prayer, since Jesus used it to teach his disciples how to pray (Luke 11:1). The prayer does, however, represent the priorities and spirit of Jesus' own prayer life and, in that sense, is the Lord's Prayer. The purpose of the prayer is to help us pray like Jesus prayed.

Study 1. Talking to the Father. Matthew 6:5-15.
Purpose: To help us grasp the nearness of God the Father.
Introduction. The Sermon on the Mount is recorded in Matthew 5—7. You might want to read the entire sermon as part of your personal preparation to lead the study.

It will help to set the tone for this study if you read Matthew 6:5-15 out loud to the group—or ask one of the group members to read it. You might even want to provide three or four different translations of the Lord's Prayer to the group, and have each one read out loud. Several versions in printable format are available at the IVP website <www.ivpress.com> under the name of this study guide.

Question 2. Jesus is not prohibiting public prayer since Jesus himself prayed publicly or out loud on a number of occasions. He is saying that personal prayer should not be done as a performance before other people. That instruction also includes boasting to other people about how long or how often we pray in secret! The best approach in public prayer is to focus on God as your single audience in prayer. That doesn't mean we ignore the people listening to our prayer. Instead we try to draw in the audience so they pray with us as we pray out loud. Planned prayers or written prayers are not "less spiritual" than spontaneous prayers. God looks at the heart of the person who prays. He is not impressed with empty words whether they are written, memorized or spontaneous.

Question 4. Mindless repetition of the Lord's Prayer is not prayer. God looks at the heart. Repeating the Lord's Prayer or the "Our Father" prayer over and over like a mantra does nothing to impress God. On the other hand, praying the Lord's Prayer privately or in unison with other believers can be a genuine, heart-felt act of worship.

Question 5. We pray because God delights in having his children come to him with their needs and concerns. God knows our needs and usually is already at work to provide those needs before we come to him. In his sovereign plan, God may use our prayers as the means of bringing about exactly what he desires.

Question 6. Reciting the Lord's Prayer personally or with other believers is a meaningful part of many worship traditions and helps us ingrain God's Word in our hearts and minds. It is also apparent that Jesus was giving this prayer as an *outline* for us to follow. He was showing us how to approach God and how to address him. He was pointing out the priorities we should have in prayer and the things we should talk to God about. Jesus wanted his followers to take his general statements and make them personal and specific to their own needs and experiences. In Luke 11 (the other occurrence of this prayer in the New Testament), Jesus' disciples said, "Teach us *to pray*"; they did not say, "Teach us *a prayer*."

Question 7. God is referred to as Father only fourteen times in the entire Old Testament—and always as the Father of the nation of Israel, never as an individual's Father. Jesus, however, addresses God only as Father. The word *Abba* is Aramaic (ara-**may**-ik)—the language spoken by the Jews in Israel in Jesus' day. It was probably the word Jesus always used to address his Father in prayer. (The only exception was Jesus' cry from the cross: "My God, my God, why have you forsaken me?" [Mt 27:6].) God is not the Father of all humanity. Only those who have believed in Jesus as Savior can claim to know God as Father: "You are all sons of God through faith in Christ Jesus" (Gal 3:26). This might be a good time to explain the gospel message briefly if you have people in your group who have not believed in Jesus.

Because of the cross, those who receive Christ's offer of salvation and cleansing are reconciled to God. We are now restored to friendship with God. But to our amazement, he raises us beyond the level of creatures or servants to the level of his own dear children.

Some people may struggle calling God "Father" because of a difficult or non-existent relationship with their own father. But even people who have had a demanding or distant father can envision the ideal father—exactly what God is.

Question 8. The use of the plural pronoun ("our Father") broadens our perspective and helps us realize that we never pray alone. We always pray (even when we pray in secret) in concert with the body of

Christ. The use of *our* also conveys a sense of belonging—we belong to God and he belongs to us; he is *our* Father. God belongs to us not in the sense that we own him or manipulate him but in the sense that an intimacy exists in our relationship.

Question 10. Our attitude in prayer always moves between a sense of closeness to God and a sense of his awesome majesty. We are on intimate terms with the sovereign king of the universe. Both aspects need to be balanced in our personal prayer and in our public worship.

Now or Later. If you include time for prayer as part of your group experience or if someone closes the study with prayer, ask those who pray to use the word *Abba* to address God.

Study 2. Showing Some Respect. Isaiah 6:1-8.

Purpose: To focus our prayers and lives on honoring God.

Introduction. Praying that God's character would be holy is like praying for a baseball to be round or water to be wet. God's name and character are intrinsically holy. We cannot add or detract in any way from that holiness. What Jesus means by this request is that God's name would be *recognized* as holy and pure, that God's character would be *treated* as sacred.

Question 2. We can honor God's name by living obediently under God's authority and Jesus' Lordship. We can also display a high regard for who God is in the way we talk about him. Another way to honor him is to be constantly aware of his presence within us and around us.

Note that Jesus' model prayer does not include a request that God would make us holy. As we invite God to hallow his character, we will live a holy life in response. Martin Luther said, "You do not command a stone that is lying in the sun to be warm. It will be warm all by itself." So when we say, "Father, there is no area of my life that you do not rule as King and Lord"—that is saying, "Hallowed be your name."

Question 3. As you explore the passage together, don't forget the feel of the floor trembling (v. 4) and the smell of the smoke (v. 4)—probably the smoke of incense that filled God's temple at the time of prayer.

Question 4. Certainly God's majesty and holiness are emphasized, but we also see God's glory and grace toward Isaiah in cleansing him and sending him to speak for God to the people. The Lord's sovereign control is reflected in Isaiah's reference to him as *King,* and his mighty power is reflected in the term "Lord Almighty."

Question 5. Exposure to God's purity and absolute separateness from sin causes Isaiah to see his own sin and the moral decay of his culture in a whole new light. When we begin to see the true glory and sacredness of God, the bright light of his purity will reveal whatever is not pleasing to him.

Question 6. The cleansing was an act of grace. Isaiah realized that he fell far short of God's purity and deserved to be excluded from God's presence, but God graciously cleansed Isaiah from sin (v. 7). The cleansing was also an act of preparation as Isaiah was called and sent out as a prophet.

Question 7. The goal of this question is not to get the members of your group to *seek* the same kind of vision that Isaiah had. The goal is to elicit the same response of self-examination because we have come to recognize the holy character of God and our own bent toward sin.

Question 9. Obedience to God always involves some level of sacrifice and giving up of our own desires and goals. "Here I am; Send me" is not just a pious phrase to be uttered in church; it is the mindset for a life of servanthood.

Question 10. Try to elicit specific and focused responses. It's easy to give a very general answer to this question: "I will live more obediently to God." Ask for specific ways that obedience will be demonstrated. Pray at the end of the study that God will help each person in the areas they desire to change.

Now or Later. Some song suggestions based on this passage are: "Holy, Holy, Holy"; "Glorify Thy Name"; "The Whole Earth Is Full of His Glory." Someone in the group may have the ability to compose a new song based on the angels' words. Remind the group as they sing that they are joining their voices with the voices of angels in heaven as God's character is lifted up and honored.

Study 3. Who's Really in Charge? Matthew 25:31-46.

Purpose: To prompt us to pray and live within the will of God.

Question 1. Biblical prayer is not a means of letting God in on our plans, but asking God to fulfill his own plans in and through us. Jesus emphasizes that our own plans are valid only to the extent that they are in accord with the eternal kingdom plans of God.

Question 2. Some students of the Lord's Prayer paraphrase this request as: "God, do what you want." This is not passive resignation but the active embrace of God's will. We know that God is gracious and good and wise, so to ask for his will is to ask for the best option.

Question 3. Some Christians believe that because God is sovereign and fully in control of his creation, everything that happens is God's will. They will say to a parent whose child has been killed in an accident, "This is God's will." That view is, in fact, a misunderstanding of God's will. God allows certain events to happen, but evil and tragedy and disaster are never his desire. God is allowing evil to run its course in our world and so tragic things happen, but do not confuse what happens in a fallen world with God's will. We are to pray that God's will would be done on earth precisely because it is not being done yet on earth.

Question 6. Entrance into God's kingdom comes by faith alone (Jn 3:3, 5). Works of compassion, however, emerge from a heart of faith. Those in the parable who fail to act in a compassionate way give evidence by that failure that they are not born again by faith in Jesus. A changed life is one of the assurances of a changed heart.

Question 8. Some interpreters believe that this judgment will be based on how a person treats the Jewish people ("these brothers of mine"). Most interpreters believe that the phrase refers to God's people in a broader sense. Ultimately how a person treats one of God's people reveals whether he is truly a believer or not. See 1 John 3:14-15.

Question 10. The parable demonstrates that our prayer for God's kingdom to come has to be translated into action. This question gives the people in your group the chance to plan specific action. You may want to suggest that they carry out their "kingdom expansion plan" as a group. See the "Now or Later" section for some ideas.

Study 4. Why Pray When You Can Worry? Luke 12:22-34.

Purpose: To give us new insight into God's provision of our needs.

Question 1. By praying for daily bread we learn daily reliance on God for our needs. We also learn to be specific in our requests to God—"Here's what I need today, Lord."

Question 2. Bread represents the necessities of life. Other necessities might include health, protection, shelter, our families, employment or peace.

Question 3. There is a difference between worry and honest concern. Worry relates to fear of the future, a mistrust that God will provide. Concern is a normal burden for the people we love and for their needs. Worry causes us to fret; concern prompts us to pray.

Question 4. Jesus certainly was not saying that we should live from hand to mouth with no concern for our future needs. He uses an extreme situation to jolt us into realizing our complete dependence on God for everything and God's gracious, abundant provision of those needs.

Question 5. Worry makes us forget our worth to God. Fear of the future and a mistrust of God and his promises make us feel as if God has forgotten us.

Question 8. Christians have a Father who actively, personally cares for our needs—and who has the ability and willingness to meet those needs. We also have God's promises of his provision and care for us as his children.

Question 10. Jesus says that our hearts will be focused wherever our treasure is. Where we invest the bulk of our treasure will become the focus of our prayers, our energy and our time.

Study 5. Costly Forgiveness. Matthew 18:21-35.

Purpose: To demonstrate how God's forgiveness of us should make us anxious to forgive others.

Group Discussion. Begin by reading the opening paragraphs out loud. Then ask for responses to the discussion question. Don't let the group settle for the "proper Christian answers." Let them struggle with the difficulty of forgiveness. The rest of Dawn's story is in the "Now or Later" section.

Question 1. We don't always feel forgiven even after coming to God and confessing (admitting) our sin. We can have confidence of our forgiveness based on God's clear promises that he is faithful to forgive us and cleanse us (1 Jn 1:9). Insecurity about forgiveness can arise from a person's misunderstanding about confession (it is admitting sin, not begging God over and over to forgive) or from a person's lack of understanding about God's gracious character and his willingness to forgive. Use the discussion time to address any insecure feelings expressed by members of the group.

Question 2. Praying that God will forgive us as we forgive others is not a contradiction of salvation and forgiveness by grace alone. We can do nothing to earn God's forgiveness. All we can do is receive it. But having been forgiven, we are now responsible to forgive. The evidence that we are truly forgiven is that we are quick to forgive.

Question 3. God's justice demanded that those who sin against God should die. Jesus, God himself, took the penalty of our sin on himself when he died on the cross. God is now free to forgive us because the penalty we deserved has been fully paid. A similar transaction takes place when we forgive someone who sins against us. We take the debt, the price, the cost, the hurt on ourselves and we release the other person from any further obligation.

Question 4. This question may open some wounds in some members of the group. Don't dwell on those difficult areas but don't ignore the hurts either. You may want to have a short prayer for someone who is hurting or talk to that person after the study time to help them begin to resolve any difficult issues.

Question 5. A talent was a huge sum of money. One talent equalled the average daily wage of a worker in the two-thirds world (about twenty dollars) times six thousand days (about twenty years). The servant owed 10,000 talents or about 2 billion dollars. It's hard to figure out how the servant got in such debt. Perhaps he was responsible to collect taxes for the king and simply squandered the money. In contrast the servant was owed the equivalent of one hundred days' wages (about five hundred dollars) by his fellow servant. I have used amounts in the question that are easier for us to relate to but the difference was dramatic. Jesus deliberately makes the debt enormous to emphasize that the servant could never, on his own, repay the debt. His only hope was forgiveness. Jesus was not, of course, trying to minimize the debt we feel when people sin against us. If anything, he was showing how deeply God feels the weight of our sin against him.

Question 6. The servant's unforgiving attitude demonstrates that he never grasped the significance and extent of his own forgiveness by the king. God's forgiveness is designed to produce humility and gratitude in those who receive it.

Question 8. Christians give different answers to the question of whether we can lose God's forgiveness. Some believe that such deliberate scorn for God's grace amounts to turning away from salvation in Christ. Other Christians believe that such an unforgiving spirit demonstrates that the person was never truly forgiven in the first place. If both positions are represented in your group let each side make its case but then move on. Be sure everyone's answer is drawn from the teaching of Scripture rather than personal opinion.

Question 9. You will get varied responses to this question. Some suggestions will be compatible with biblical teaching and some may not. Have the group talk about each suggestion. A few possibilities for answers: write a letter rather than talk face to face, ask a mutual friend to go with you to mediate, break off the relationship and go on with life, look for ways to get even.

Question 11. The group members can help each other form biblical strategies for dealing with people who are difficult to forgive. You may want to assign accountability partners to encourage each other to carry through on specific plans that are made.

Study 6. Tackling Temptation. John 17:6-19.

Purpose: To cause us to take seriously our vulnerability to temptation and to rely on God's resources to overcome the temptation.

Question 2. These phrases in the Lord's Prayer ask God not to allow us to come under the sway of temptation so strongly that it overpowers us and causes us to sin. William Barclay paraphrases like this: "Do not deliver me helpless into temptation's power" (*The Lord's Prayer* [Louisville, Ky.: Westminster John Knox, 1998], p. 104). Martin Luther wrote: "We cannot help being exposed to [Satan's] assaults, but we pray that we may not perish under them."

Question 3. Some group members may question the reality of Satan—a personal tempter. Both the New Testament writers and Jesus himself consistently affirm Satan's existence and power. God is greater than Satan and sovereignly rules over Satan, but Satan is still a powerful enemy.

Question 4. The disciples had come to know that Jesus had come from the Father and that he was all that he claimed to be. They had also come to a point of confidence in their relationship with Jesus. Their commitment to Jesus was about to be severely tested, but Jesus prays that they might remain faithful to him.

Question 5. During his ministry on earth, Jesus had acted as the protector of his disciples. Jesus asks in this prayer that the Father would now assume that role while Jesus endured his arrest and crucifixion. Ultimately, Jesus returned to heaven and the Holy Spirit took that responsibility (see Eph 6:10-18).

Question 6. Jesus had given them the Father's words of assurance that they could rely on in the difficult hours ahead. They could also remember that Jesus had prayed this prayer for them and that the Father would answer Jesus' prayer by protecting them.

Question 8. If we were taken out of the world or totally protected from temptation, our commitment to Jesus would be untested commitment. God uses testing to strengthen our "muscle" of obedience and to produce Christ-like character in us. But testing also brings with it the possibility of failure and even of abandoning our commitment to Jesus. Judas had heard and seen all that the other disciples had heard and seen but, while they were becoming committed followers of Christ, he was becoming an instrument of the evil one.

Question 9. Try not to allow the discussion of this question to focus on "rules." Keep the emphasis on our separation from sinful behavior and a whole-hearted commitment to God.

Study 7. The Power and Glory. Revelation 4.

Purpose: To experience genuine worship as a response and conclusion to prayer.

Question 3. God the Father has no physical body or form. He is spirit. Jesus is the only member of the Trinity to take on physical form. John sees only the likeness of the form of a human being on the throne. The throne represents the center of God's revealing of himself. The scene certainly portrays God's purity and transcendent majesty as well as God's willingness to reveal himself to us.

Question 4. The elders join with the angels in lifting praise and worship to God. Angels worship God as their Creator and sovereign King. Human beings also worship God as their Redeemer and Savior. The crowns of reward that we will receive for our faithfulness to Christ in this life will be laid before the Father in humble acknowledgment of his grace.

Question 5. Will you find prisons or criminal courts in God's perfect world? What kinds of entertainment will be available? How about hospitals or nursing homes—or funeral homes?

Question 6. When we worship privately or in community, we are joining our voices and hearts with the angels of God and with millions of believers already in heaven. That perspective makes even a small gathering of believers significant.

Question 7. The early Christians who first read this book saw the power of the Roman Empire unleashed against them in persecution. This scene helped them realize that God was still in control and that his authority was greater than any human authority.

Question 9. Genuine worship is not prompted so much by external, up-front changes as it is by a receptive and open heart to God. Certainly those in leadership can help stimulate worship by their choice of music and other elements of worship, by their own humility before God, and by words of instruction or encouragement that draw a congregation upward. The key to God-centered worship, however, is the focus of our hearts on him. When we sing, we sing to him; when we pray, we pray to him; our expressions of praise and adoration are for his pleasure and exaltation.

Study 8. A Passion for Prayer. Luke 11:1-13.

Purpose: To gain new understanding of God's gracious attitude toward us when we pray.

Question 1. Some of the words and phrases included in Matthew's version of the Lord's Prayer are missing in Luke's version. In the New International Version the following words or phrases do not appear: "our"; "in heaven"; "your will be done on earth as it is in heaven"; "deliver us from the evil one." Some later New Testament manuscripts (and some of our translations) do include all or some of those phrases. The words were probably added by later copyists who imported them from Matthew's Gospel. The "missing" phrases should not be a concern. Jesus is giving the prayer in Luke in a different context and at a different time than he did in Matthew. Jesus includes the phrases that are relevant to this particular context.

Question 2. On a purely human level, Jesus shows that even the grumpiest neighbor will respond to our need if we persist long enough in making our request. Jesus goes on to point out that our Father responds much more readily and willingly to our need than any neighbor.

Question 4. Jesus is giving a general overview of God's attitude toward us when we pray. He is *not* saying that God will give us anything we ask for. These verses have to be read in context with everything else Jesus taught about prayer. Sometimes what we ask for is not in line with God's kingdom reign in our lives or it doesn't bring glory to God's character or it will not really meet the need we think we have at the moment. In those situations God may say "no" to what we ask—or we may have to wait a while before God's "yes" answer comes. Jesus' point in these verses is that God is anxious to respond to us.

Question 5. Sometimes these verses are quoted completely out of context as if we can ask for anything and get it from God. But God is not a vending machine or a cosmic Santa Claus. He is a Father who knows and desires the best for his children.

Question 6. If a father gave his hungry child a scorpion to chew on instead of an egg, we would be horrified. So, if fathers (who have sinful hearts) have the desire to bless their children, why do we doubt that God is anxious to bless us?

Question 7. It may seem at times that God gives us something hurtful instead of something good, but the problem is our limited perception not God's goodness. Jesus said that fathers (especially the heavenly Father) know how to give *good gifts* to their children.

Question 8. Those who have prayed a long time about an issue need to realize that God is not being cruel by saying "no" or "not yet" to a request. He may have other purposes to accomplish in our lives and in the lives of others before he grants our request. Our job is to keep asking—and to keep trusting in the goodness of the Father's heart.

Douglas Connelly (MDiv and MTh, Grace Theological Seminary) is the senior pastor at Davison Missionary Church, near Flint, Michigan. He is also the author of Angels Around Us *(InterVarsity Press) and* The Bible for Blockheads *(Zondervan) as well as seventeen LifeBuilder Bible Studies.*